Picnic on the Moon

For Wendy

Brian Morse.

BRIAN MORSE

Picnic on the Moon

Illustrated by Joep Bertrams

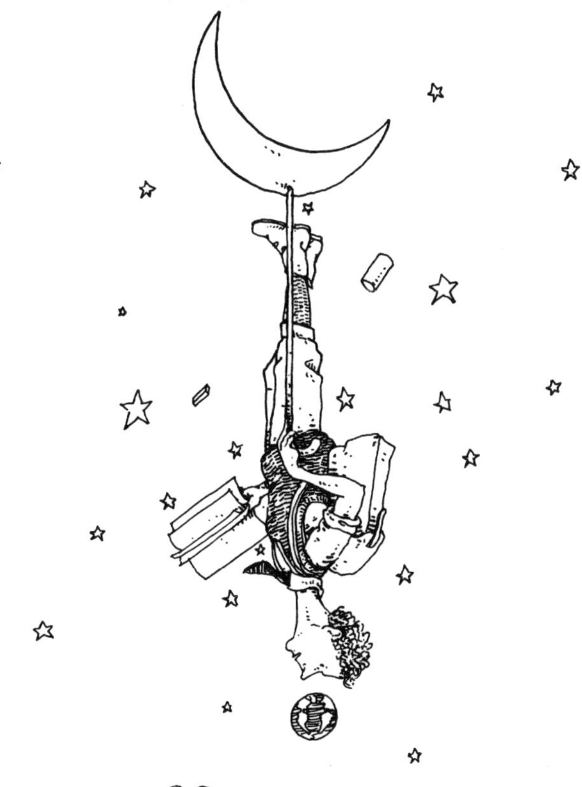

TURTON & CHAMBERS

First published 1990

Turton & Chambers Ltd
Station Road, Woodchester
Stroud, Glos GL5 5EQ, England
and 10 Armagh Street
Victoria Park, Perth
Western Australia 6100

Typesetting by Avonset
Midsomer Norton, Bath
Printed in England by
Short Run Press, Exeter

British Library
Cataloguing in Publication Data
Morse, Brian, 1949–
Picnic on the Moon
I. Title II. Bertrams, Joep
823'.914

ISBN 1 872148 00 X

CONTENTS

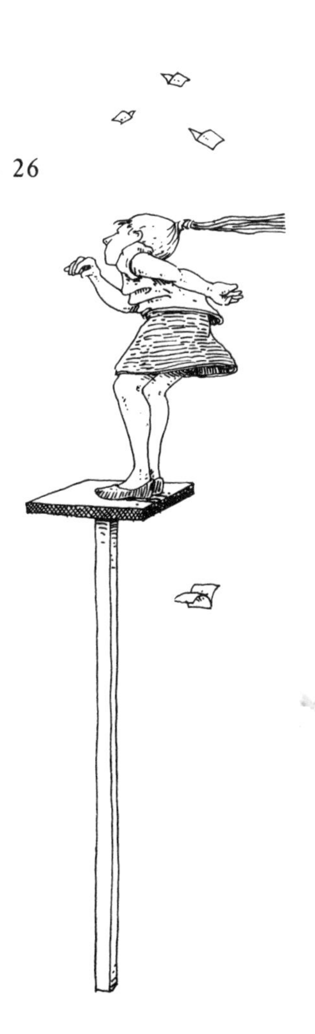

CRACK-A-DAWN

Good day and good morning!
Here is your early morning tea
and here are your crack-a-dawn cereals.
Sugar is also provided.
Breakfast in bed, room service calling!
Are you awake?

Darren, sit up! I'm giving you
ten seconds, starting now! TEN.
The weather outside is fine – at least
by North Sea standards. NINE.
Just a fresh Force Six blowing and a spot
of rain lashing the rooftops. EIGHT.
The sun is shining – lucky Australians!
The bus, however, is on time
according to local radio – SEVEN –
and if you want to walk again and be
reported to the Head that is your business
but – SIX – I have a bus to catch too
and you can pay for a taxi out of your pocket money
if I miss it the third morning running.
FIVE. Your gerbil has been eaten by the dog
and the dog has been eaten by a crocodile
that got in down the chimney and is, at this moment,
opening its jaws over your toes –
feel it? No? Oh well.
FOUR. A letter has just arrived,
postmarked Wembley, inviting you to play
for England next Saturday against Czechoslovakia –
bet you won't be late for that. THREE.
Czechoslovakia was one of the eighteen spellings
wrong in your Geography homework.

Why wasn't it handed in last week? I found
the letter you forged from your dad
stating you had a dental appointment
on Friday afternoon – TWO – you could
at least have spelt his Christian name right
and the address. Make an appointment with him
an hour after you intend to go out tonight.

ONE. This is your mother speaking
and I am about to pour your tea
over your head, even if it causes me
extra washing. I won't begrudge the powder.
Darren, I'm giving you HALF A SECOND, A QUARTER,
AN EIGHTH. No this is not a nightmare,
no the trickle of water you feel at this moment
is NOT an illusion . . .

I CAN'T SAY THAT

Dear Auntie Beryl,
Thanks for the Christmas present.
It was lovely –
except twenty-four-piece puzzles are much too easy
for my age.
Mum's put it away for the baby.
I can't say that.

Dear Pen Pal,
Thanks for your letter.
You've got very nice handwriting.
Your holiday in the Bahamas sounded smashing.
We went to Weston this year
and it rained every single minute
except the afternoon we were going home.
I can't say that.

Dear Santa,
There's a whole string of presents
I'd really like to have
But why were the only ones I got last year
the little ones?
I can't say that.

Dear Teacher,
I think it's a very good idea
to practise writing letters,
but I already know
where to put the address and the date
and the postcode and the 'Yours sincerely',
and the 'With love from' –
it's the bit in between I find difficult.
I can't say that.

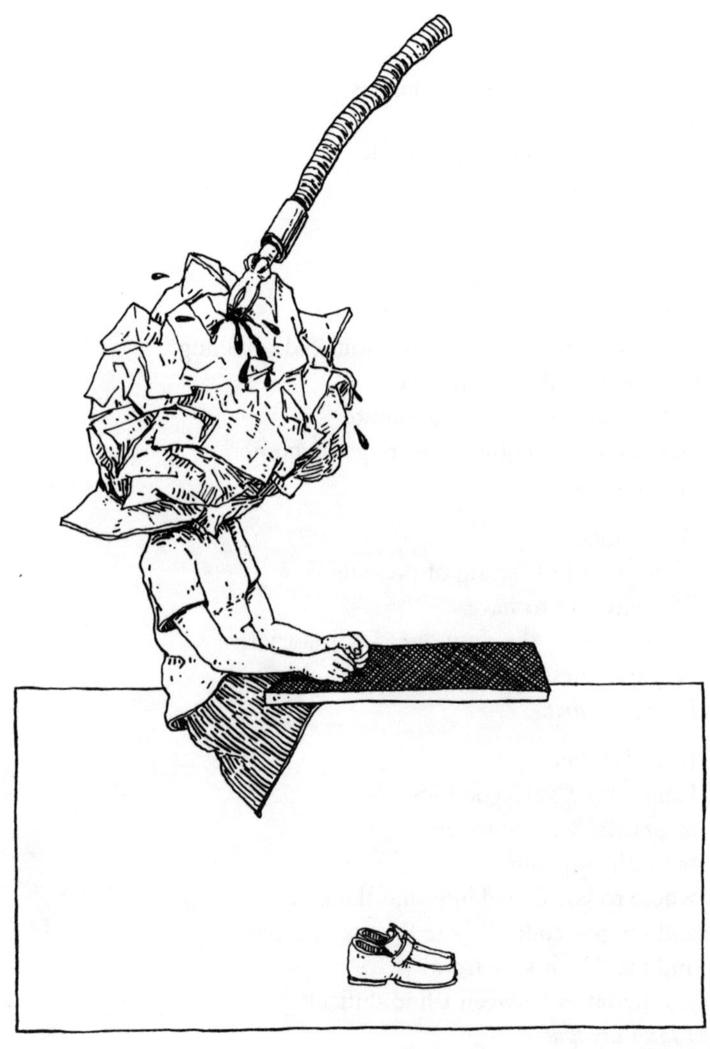

WRITE A POEM ABOUT A FRIEND

Hayley is a nice person.
At playtime she is my friend
and during lessons I help her.
She is no good at sums
and can't spell proper.
She has little blue eyes
and she eats too much.
When she yells she goes all red,
her face swells up,
her eyes pop,
and she tells LIES –
like wen she came bak from
play jus now
and sed Im not yore frend no more
yuv a bad temper
i saw what you writ
Well im not yore frend neather
your NASTY Haily!!!

A good start, Justine,
but for some reason
your spelling went off towards the end.

PETS' DAY

Pets' day.
Let's sit on the carpet and discuss
our pets
and the ones we can bring to school,
the sensible ones,
gerbils, rabbits, hamsters.
No dogs or cats, sorry.
Guinea pigs yes, horses no.
If anyone hasn't got a pet they can bring a teddy.

Now has anyone got an unusual pet?
At his last school the Head
had a girl with a baby elephant.
Okay, laugh all you want
but he swears it's true.
Very funny, Sonya, but now the joke's over.

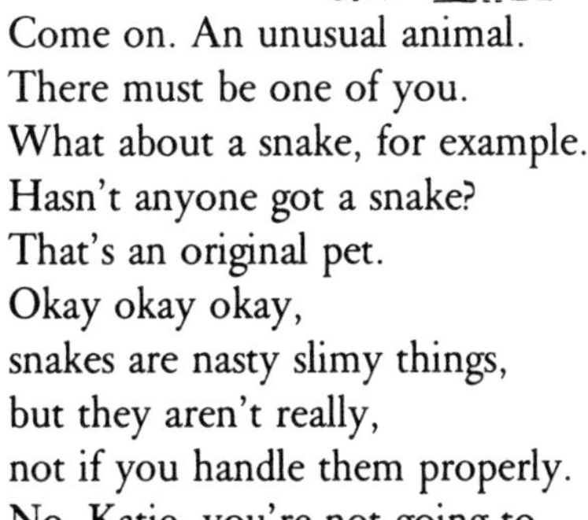

Come on. An unusual animal.
There must be one of you.
What about a snake, for example.
Hasn't anyone got a snake?
That's an original pet.
Okay okay okay,
snakes are nasty slimy things,
but they aren't really,
not if you handle them properly.
No, Katie, you're not going to
be made to touch it.

No one? Well, what about tortoises?
Ah, I knew there'd be lots of tortoises.
You, Christopher, what's that?
You've got a snake after all.
You have!
That's really exciting!
I didn't know.
How've you hidden it from me all this time!
Can you bring it in?
You're not sure?
That's a shame.
Well, you can always ask.
I'll write a note straightaway.
I could fetch it in my car.
What kind is it?
A boa? A python?
You don't know.
You really don't?

Well, where do you keep it?
Outside in the garden?
In a shed? In a cage?
In nothing really – isn't that a bit dangerous?
Oh, it isn't a dangerous snake.
Well, is it an English snake?
We've had some very bad weather recently.
Most snakes people keep as pets
need lots of heat.
You keep them in a special heated glass cage.
No, Katie, you won't need to be here
if Christopher brings it in.

Christopher, come on, tell us,
I'm a bit mystified.
Where did this snake come from?
Did your mum and dad go out and buy it
or was it a present?
Oh, neither of those –
it sort of happened along – appeared by the tree,
climbed up the branches.
It hisses but it isn't dangerous.
It eats grass
hanging from the bottom branch
and runs up the tree if you get too close.
Perhaps it thinks it's back in the jungle!
It would certainly feel at home
in this room at the moment.
Mark! How many times do I have to tell you –
do not do that!

Christopher, now about this snake.
Why don't you bring your mother in
and she and I can have a little talk?

He lives with his dad in the flats, sir.
He lives with his dad in the flats, sir.
He hasn't any garden.
He hasn't any tree.
He hasn't any snake.
He hasn't anything, sir.

CLIVE COTTER

The new boy –
Clive Cotter –
broke my pencil,
hid my rubber.

Moved my chair
and made me fall,
wrote my name
on the toilet wall.

Terror of the playground,
worst that you'll meet –
Clive Cotter,
the dirty rotter.

Called me a liar,
made me a fool,
took my crisps,
broke every rule.

But now he's my friend!
My best friend!
How did it happen?
A fight

in the playground
neither could win,
both kept in –
be friends you two!

I fought him,
Clive fought me,
his mother invited me
home to tea!

Terrors of the street,
worst that you'll meet –
two dirty rotters,
two Clive Cotters!

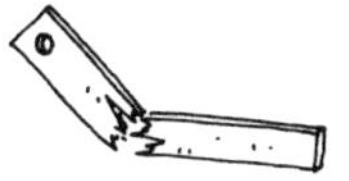

ONE OF OUR RUBBERS IS MISSING

Ladies and gentlemen,
one of our rubbers is missing,
a blue pencil rubber
used twice or thrice
before morning break
and never seen again.

Now this class has a very good record,
only two 10ps and an anorak
disappeared in mysterious circumstances
in a term and a half.
Search your consciences, check your pockets.

No result? A shame.
I was hoping not to have to use
my Sherlock Holmes act
so early in the week.
I suppose I better look for suspects
before I begin turning out coat linings.

Ah, a development! Nicola thinks
she saw the rubber
after play after all.
Well, she is the expert –
it was hers.
Where was it, Nicola?
Come on! No need to be shy.
You lent it to Richard.
What has Richard to say?
She didn't. Didn't what?
Oh, didn't lend it.

Ladies and gentlemen,
this is turning into
one of the most difficult cases
this teacher-detective has ever dealt with.
Quiet a moment! Who shouted out that
Nicola never had the rubber in the first place?
Ah, Kerry. You. Stand up a moment.
An interesting theory.
What's that, Lisa?
Silence a moment.
Ah, Kerry has a blue rubber
in her desk too? She has?
May we see it?
Thank you, Kerry. I see,
a blue Mickey Mouse rubber,
just like yours, Nicola.
Well, Kerry, it's very well preserved
if Father Christmas gave you it
two months ago.

I see. Your mother wouldn't let you
bring it to school till today.
Very wise of her I might say.

Now, Kerry, there's no reason to cry.
No one's accusing you of anything
yet. Yes
I'm quite sure your dad will back you up.
And there's no reason for you to cry, Nicola,
either. I think it ought to be me crying.
In fact I think I am.
Am what? Crying!

Now listen, Kerry,
isn't there the faintest chance
you left your immaculate rubber
at home?
None.
Well that's pretty definite.
Now what about you, Nicola?
Might you by any chance . . .
No.
Richard, you're trying to say something.
What's that?

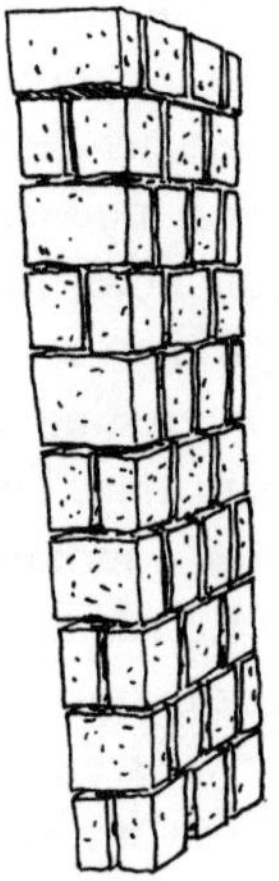

Richard, let's get this clear.
Nicola lent you the rubber
and you lent the rubber to Kerry
who said she was going to keep it
and would bash you up if you let on –
duff you over – it's more or less the same thing.
Sorry, Hayley, dear – what did you say?
That you saw Kerry bring the rubber
to school this morning.
You're quite sure?
No honestly,
there's no reason to fetch the class Bible.

KNOCK KNOCK KNOCK
Yes, do come in.
Oh, hello, headmaster.
No, no trouble at all.
Just bashing my head against a brick wall.

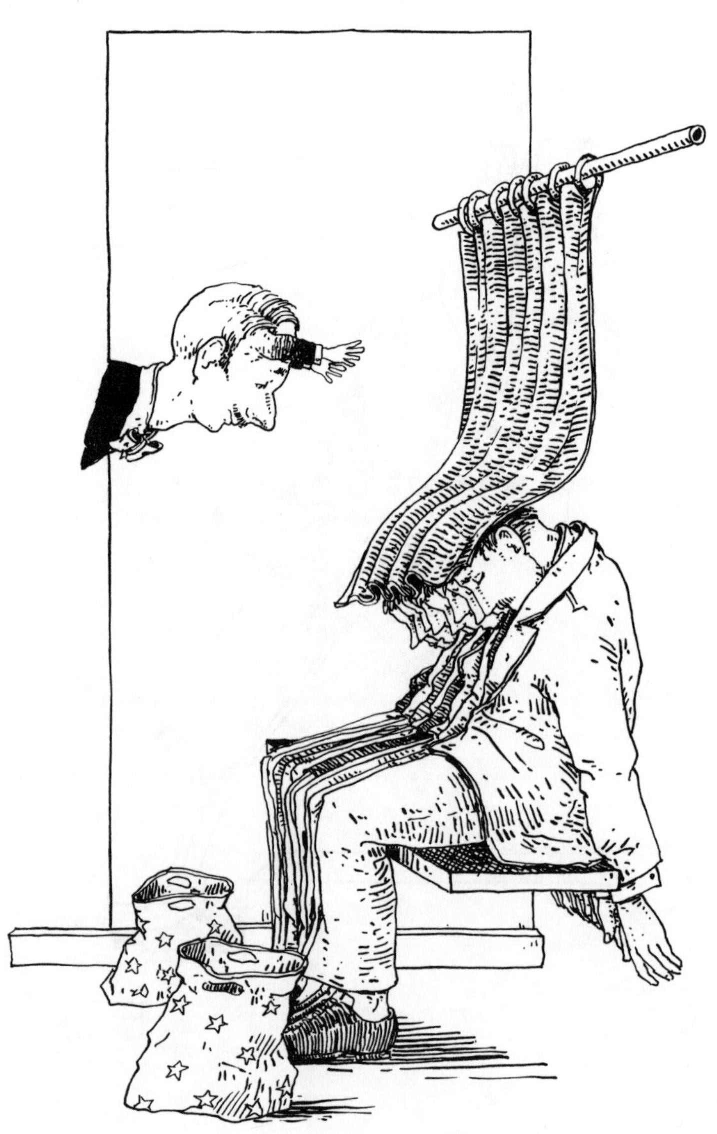

A BIT OF A DEVIL

To Lisa

The headmaster rubbed his hands in glee.
'Now sit still, kids, and listen to me.
We've an entertainer coming – be as good as you can
for he's promised princesses and dragons,
castles and ghosts, magic and mystery,
the most stupendous fun.
I and all the teachers are really looking forward to it.'

The entertainer came in. He was dressed in black.
We dared not breathe. We were as quiet as mice.
He carried in his props – two plastic shopping bags.
You could see the teachers wondering – is that all?
Then he turned. His smile was devilish!

'Children, I've a disappointment. I'm afraid
this show isn't suitable for adults.
Perhaps your teachers better have a little snooze.'
We cheered. The teachers' heads drooped.

Then we had what he'd promised – and more, much more,
a magic circle of fire, a dinosaur roaring in a storm,
a trip through space – it went on for hours!

At the end, he woke the headmaster up
(he'd snored the whole time).

The headmaster called for three hearty cheers.
'It was the best show I've ever seen,' he said.
'The time passed like a dream.'

JAMES HAD A MAGIC SET FOR CHRISTMAS

James had practised the tricks for days
but in front of the class
they all went wrong.
The invisible penny
dropped from his sleeve,
the secret pocket
failed to open,
his magic wand broke.
'Perhaps another time,' Miss Burroughs suggested,
'another day
when you've the hang of it.'

'No, Miss! Please!
I can do them, honestly.'

Suddenly
a white rabbit was sitting
on Miss Burroughs' table,
a green snake, tongue flicking,
scattered the class from the carpet,
the school was showered with golden coins
that rolled into piles on the playground.
'But, James!' Miss Burroughs said. 'Shouldn't – '
There was a flash of lightning.

While the fire brigade coaxed
Miss Burroughs down from the oak
she'd flown into
on the other side of the playground,
the caretaker quietly swept up the mess
and Mr Pinner, the headmaster,
confiscated the magic set.
'A rather dangerous toy,' he said, 'James!'

James is still asking for it back.

PAINT

I should like to paint
the eye of a raindrop
the foot of a thunderclap
the heart of a cloud

the roving eye of dew
clawed foot of lightning
the elastic heart of cumulus

paint
a mascara-ed eye
a sultry heart
a silken foot

then
black cloud
forked lightning
a splintered raindrop

a squall of rain
wet hair on a brow
a dubious eye

a finger of rain walking across a sodden field to
a fringe of wood where a majestic tree is falling

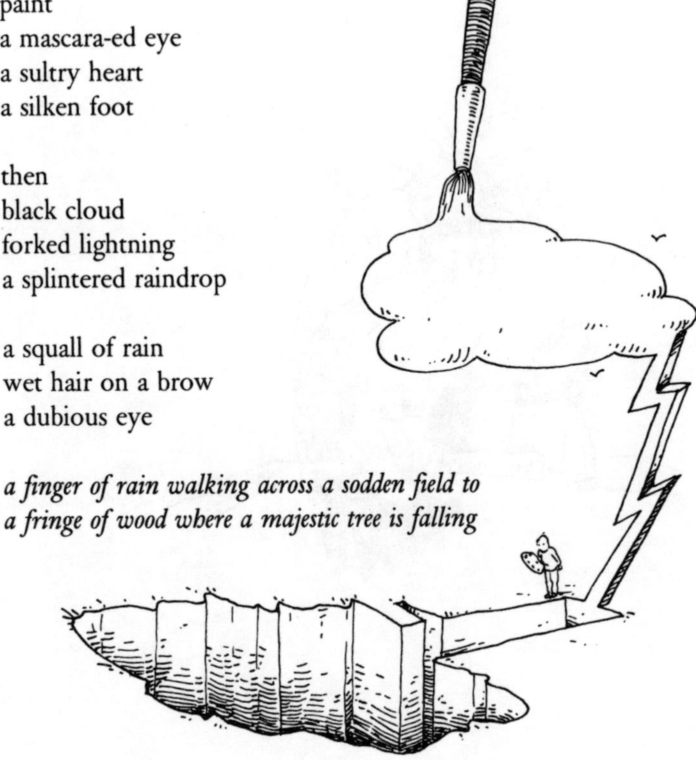

TOO MUCH STORY

For today's story
I imagined the wind caught me
and swept me skywards.
But at play I imagined harder than I meant,
the wind came hustling and bustling
and a great windy palm and fingers
slid under my legs and bottom
and before I could shout out help!
I was above the ground.

Then I shouted – did I shout! –
but only a five-year-old
playing aeroplanes by the drain cover
heard.
And he just watched me fly –
a quiet one him! –
till I was a dot in the sky
and his class went in.

Oh well, you get used to living on air
and learn to swim on its billows,
even though the heart-strings tear
when you think those you miss don't care
and you know that one day
the five-year-old will turn six then seven
and will forget to wave
from his bedroom window.
Then you'll feel lonely, won't you?

BETCHA

Betcha can't jump!
Betcha I could!
No one could jump!
Betcha I can!

How could anyone be so stupid
Mum said in hospital that evening
as to attempt the world long jump record
between two slippery roofs
of different levels
with no run up
and the sun in your eyes?
Big question mark
against your sanity.
She cried. It was the worst moment.

Egged on by best mate Tony Maynes
in an attempt to impress
Lisa Harrison
it was much too easy.

But Lisa Harrison's not visiting me –
I'm not sure she even knows who I am –
and Tony says
I never thought you'd be so crazy.
Do you know how many dinner-times and breaks
I've missed because of you?
My Mum says you're a bad influence.
I'm to keep away.
I better go actually,
the buses are only every hour and a half.

Now I climb the monkey-frames
of the apparatus that tethers
my leg to the hospital ceiling.
I'm a Tarzan in pyjamas.

Nurse Atkins says she's never seen
such a performer.
Just mind you don't break your leg!

THE KEYS

When I was ten years old
Mum got a job.
I was given THE KEYS.

They dangled on a keyring
that said West Park Garage in golden letters.
Dad said DON'T lose them
whatever you do.

Wow!
I had THE KEYS!

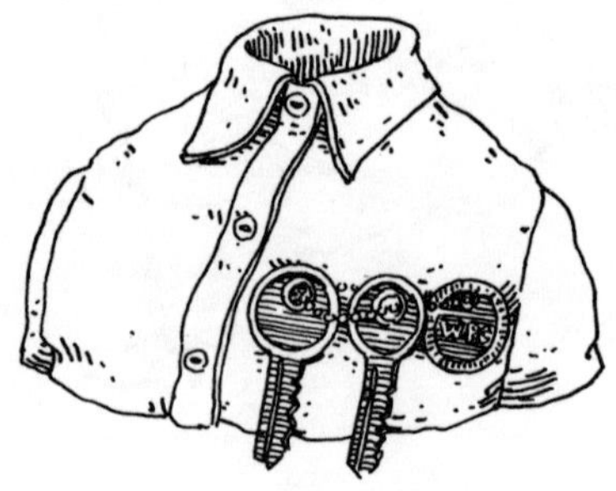

It was an enormous responsibility
Mum said,
fixing my eye
and bringing me back down to earth with a bump.
The house was in my care,
I was to come straight back home from school,
use the keys to let myself in,
shut the door after,
no speaking to strangers,
nothing silly

you wouldn't do when I was around
(What about the usual silly things?
Are you LISTENING, Dad said!),
nobody in,
watch the telly till I get back,
do your homework.
I'll be straight home.
Your dad gets in at seven.
If for any reason
you need us
our work numbers are
behind the kitchen clock
and an emergency five pound note
(an *emergency*, mind you) –
or there's always Mrs Billingham
down the street –
a real emergency!

At first the telephone
used to greet me
as I came through the door.
Had a nice day, love?
I'll be on time tonight.
What made you late?
I've already phoned twice.

At first I used to watch the telly
(Switch off and unplug it
when you've finished)
right through from the end of Play School
to the Six O'Clock News.
(Put the kettle on for tea.
That would be really nice of you.
Make sure there's enough water in it.)

If anyone called
I was OUT
or at least NOT IN –
which put paid to friends.
After a bit I left the front door open
in case the phone rang
(You sound puffed.
Is anything the matter?)
but Mum came home early once,
caught me in the street
and that was the end of that.
If I can't trust you on your own
I'll just have to give up the job.
You like the extra pocket-money, don't you?
I got the message.

Then the nights began to draw in,
soon it was getting dark
before six.
They changed the clocks
and made it dark
earlier and earlier.

Not much fun now,
the house empty and cold,
I began to not like it so much.

One night I was watching a film
on Channel Four,
some creepy old thriller,
nothing special, really just kids' stuff,
when I suddenly realized
it was late –
no Mum,

way past six,
creeping towards quarter past.
Dad was doing overtime.
Where on earth had she got to?

The time began to rush towards half past.
I went into the kitchen
and put the kettle on.
Still no Mum.
I looked out through the front curtains.
No sign of her.
A few cars swishing in the rain.
A woman with an umbrella.
Where was she?
Had something happened to her?

I began to imagine all kinds of things –
road accidents, a robbery at her works,
someone had kidnapped her.

I watched the end of the film.
I was just beginning to go up the stairs
to the toilet
when I heard this noise
from up there,

only a little noise,
a click it might have been,
not much more than that,
but it shouldn't have been there.
I stopped dead.
I thought of the film.
Very carefully I edged downstairs
then ran
and put all the lights on,
every one,
even the pantry light
that didn't light anything
except the potatoes and ironing-board,
and stood in the hall near the front door
with my key in the lock,
ready to escape if need be,
listening for the noise
and watching the bend of the stairs.

Mum.
Where had she got to?
I kept thinking of that film.

After a bit when nothing happened
I went and sat in the living room,
with the television off,
just the swish of the rain outside,
waiting,
just sitting there
waiting for the two noises,
Mum's key in the door
and that noise from upstairs.

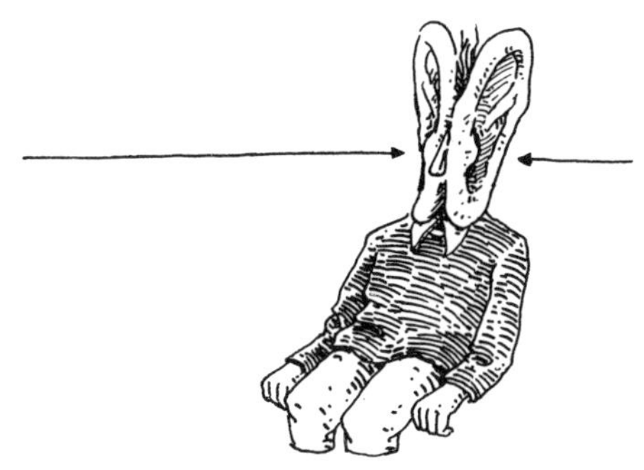

Five minutes passed.
Ten.
I must have imagined it.

Then the noise came again,
a terrible creaking and groaning,
a real noise this time –
spine-chilling!
I ran out of the living room
down the hall
through the door,
outside.

The front door slammed behind me.
I'd left my keys inside.
Who cared?
I wasn't going back in there again
with that inside!

It was raining cats and dogs.
I was soaked in a second.

I went down the front path
The house was blazing with lights
like the *Titanic* heading for disaster.

As I stood on the drive
I could see something moving about inside the house.
My blood froze.
I'd been right.
There had been something.
But what?
I had to see.
I crept back
closer and closer,
ready to scream
Murder! Police!

It was Mum, in her dressing gown.

After a while she came to the door
rubbing her eyes
and peered out.
I came up the steps.

What on earth are you doing out there?
What are your keys doing in the door?
Why are all the lights on?
They cost a fortune.
Didn't you see my note by the kettle?
I had a splitting headache, terrible.
Mr Johnson sent me home early.
I went to bed.
I've been asleep most of the afternoon.

What did you think I felt
when I woke up
and found you missing?
It was terrible.

You're wet through,
dripping.
What on earth's going on?
I hope this isn't the kind of thing you always get up to
when I'm out at work.

Then I remembered the note.
I'd thought it was a shopping-list.
I hadn't bothered to read it.

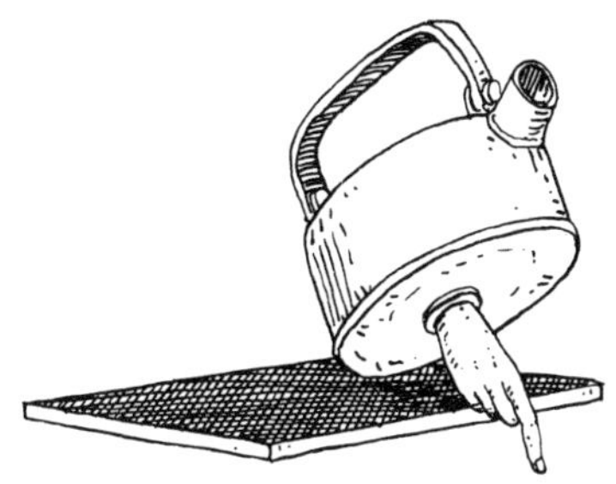

THE QUARREL

When Dad and our next-door neighbour quarrelled
Mum came out to add a few choice words.
('You definitely didn't hear that,' Dad told me.)
Then his front door slammed and our back.
Curtains twitched all down the street.

Now he avoids us.
When the milkman comes to be paid
no one leans over the fence to save him the walk.
'What's up with you silly lot?' the milkman says.
'You'd think you weren't speaking.'

The dustbins go out separately,
no more 'good mornings' and 'how's your cough?'.
'I know we were in the right,' Dad says.
'Even his wife said so.
But it's a pity it came to shouting.'

I met him the other day with his dogs.
He didn't look at me straight.
'Mr Thompson – ' I began but his eyes went past me
and he pulled savagely at the dogs
which began to bark and jump.

I felt like kicking him – I used to walk those dogs.
I felt like screaming at him,
'I thought you were all right
till you turned out stupid.
You were only pretending to be nice.

'And it wasn't my fault. I didn't do a thing.'
(Everyone else has forgotten what caused the quarrel.)
But we both went on walking.
I wish I'd kicked him.
That would have set the curtains twitching.

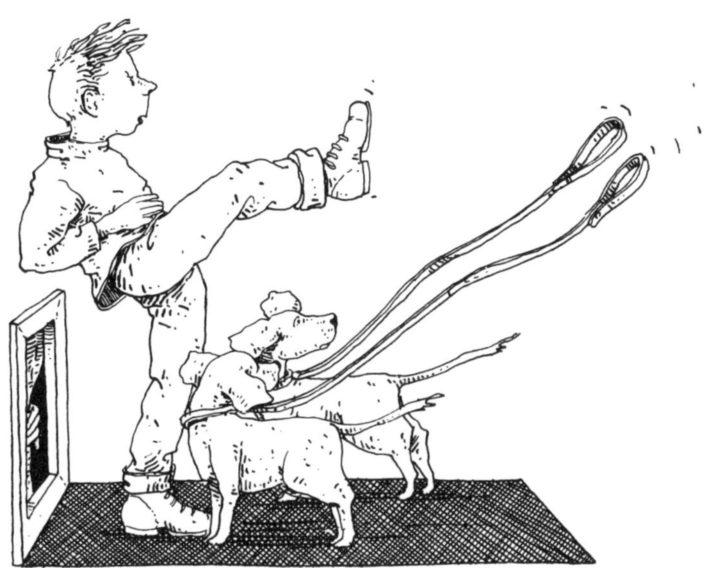

D.I.Y. MAN

Dad's a hobbyist, a hobby man.
Every moment he can
is spent on his latest fad,
ruling his life, driving us mad.

He's been into computers, and cars,
and home-made wine in enormous jars.
His latest is tropical freshwater fish –
they're the answer to his fairy godmother's wish.

The garden's a desert, a waste,
since herbaceous borders became his taste.
Nine times out of ten we have to catch the bus –
he blames losing the car manual on us.

The sight of a new magazine is a sad
and certain sign that yet again he's got it bad.
'Your family's an abandoned hobby,' Mum sighs.
'Let's face it we could have turned into flies

on the wall of that shed you bought
for the fancy pigeons which caught
your eye at that show. And as for the hi-fi it's the same –
Hey! Are you listening? Do you remember my name?'

'Pardon?' Dad says, ever so politely,
raising his head. 'A new idea's just struck me.'

THE NIGHT KITCHEN

The radio alarm woke me in the night.
It shouted, 'Come on, sleepy-head!
The moon's out and shining!
How long are you staying in bed?'

As I groped my way downstairs
(the lights were on strike)
the electric toothbrush buzzed out of the bathroom
like a wasp on a bike.

In the hall the phone was chatting
to its opposite number in Carlisle,
and the hair-curlers had given
the curtains the latest hair style.

And the kitchen! In there
the toaster was tapping on the bread-bin,
and its friend the electric carving knife
was sawing its way in,

the can-opener had opened
enough cat-food for a week,
and the garbage disposal unit
was giving a delighted squeak.

I fled back to bed,
chased by the toothbrush,
hid beneath the sheets
and began counting sheep in a rush.

Oh no, it's beginning once more!
What's this I hear?
The microwave beginning to dance?
The fridge-freezer offering me a lift to France?

TOAST GHOSTS

We don't have ghosts in our house. That noise
is just Mum creeping downstairs for crisps in the dark.

In the hall she puts the light on to avoid the Hoover
so you know it's her and not – well, you know.

Then you hear Dad waking and groaning,
'What on earth!' and out of bed he gets too.

And here's Mum at the bottom of the stairs
with her rustling bag of crisps whispering ever so loud:

'Why are you up? I didn't mean to wake you,'
and Dad says, resigned, 'The bed was cold.

And what's the use of dieting in the day
if you eat all night?' 'I was hungry,' Mum says.

(You'd think by now she'd got a better answer than that
but she hasn't.) 'The whole point about dieting is,'

Dad says, 'but I won't expand.'
'I'll go without my breakfast,' Mum says, 'honestly.'

'I bet,' Dad says and goes downstairs too.
By now my elder sister Tracey has woken

and is stumbling to the toilet. She slams the door
and slams it on the way back and slams her own door.

'Listen! You've woken Tracey up,' Dad says very clearly.
'You know what she's like in the morning

if she doesn't get her beauty sleep. Venomous!
The next thing – oh speak of the devil!' That's me.

'Haven't I ever told you – ONCE IN BED STAY THERE?
Do you know what time it is?' 'You woke me,' I say

in my sleepy little kid's voice that sometimes fools him.
Luckily the canaries choose that moment to start chirping

their morning chorus. The kettle boils. 'Tea or coffee?'
Dad asks. 'I think I might have beans,' Mum says

like something exotic. By now I'm loading up the toaster.
'I've got to be up in six hours,' Dad grumbles.

'Two sugared, one with saccharin. I'll have three slices
with butter – none of that slimming margarine nonsense.'

'Me too,' Mum says. 'I'll go back on my diet tomorrow.'
'The day after tomorrow,' Dad yawns. 'The day after.'

A MIDNIGHT THUNDERCLAP

A midnight thunderclap wakes me. I lie very still, a small baboon in a primeval forest. What woke me? What on earth could it have been?

A rain-drop drips from branch to earth outside the window, then a silent silver explosion fills the room. Its noise runs from one end of the street to the other and back again. My skin's radar, it feels the explosion come up past the Moores', past the Sanghas', past the Rocks', past the Fullwoods', and in the next bedroom a light goes on and is hastily switched off again. The air's like a too-long-left-on electric blanket and I want to throw off the covers and hide under the covers and –

Then suddenly it's silent and very dark. Over, all over, gone. I raise my head. The rain-drop drips again, twice, quickly, as if to get it done with, as if something might notice it, attract attention.

A voice in the next room says, 'Is the window open? For goodness sake did you remember to unplug?' But suddenly we're back in the forest, full of light again, which leaps at me leering and steps back in less time than it took the rain-drop, not even time to cower before the top-most branches part and the tree-trunk writhes, tries to uproot itself, footsteps of the searching thunder crash to and fro above me crashing, crashing, no nonsense this time, IT'S ME IT'S AFTER.

Then all over again. Finished again. All over again. Wait. *Wait.*

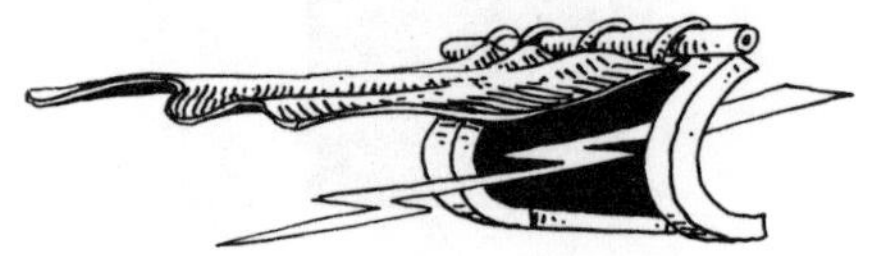

VICTORIA SPONGE

Cream the margarine and sugar,
six ounces of each –
that's right.
Add three eggs
with a little flour,
one at a time –
you're doing fine.
Okay, tip the rest of the flour in.
Mix it till it's smooth
and just drops from the spoon.

Well done!
That's perfection!

Now the best bit –
cleaning the bowl.
Scrape it clean.
Get every last blob
including the one on the end of your nose!

What a shame
it's only a cake!

DIFFERENCE OF TASTE

Hurry curry, spinach omelette,
pork with leeks, charcoaled chicken,
sweet and sour, peanut kurma –
all I eat's tomato soup

You tear the packet, pour the water, stir –
all I eat's tomato soup

Winter pudding, lobster pâté,
chick pea salad, mushroom cocktail,
Murgh Mussalam, veal with quince –
all I eat's tomato soup

You tear the packet, pour the water, stir –
all I eat's tomato soup

Have a taste then – just a trifle –
spoonful – spit it – do you good –
big strong boy/girl – back in my day –
all I eat's tomato soup

You tear the packet, pour the water, stir –
all I eat's tomato soup

Frogs with sweetcorn, slugs in aspic,
devilled cobra, eel on toast,
prunes with custard, slime and gunge,
all I eat's tomato soup –

You tear the packet, pour the water, stir –
all I eat's tomato soup

A PERFECTIONIST

What's that noise? my friend Graham asked.
It sounds like it's coming from upstairs,
a rumble like a goods train
labouring up an embankment
and never quite reaching the top.

That? Oh that!
You get used to that.
It's only Dad snoring,
I said.

But I can hear it above the telly
and the computer game
and your sister's record,
and the plane going overhead!
Graham complained.
Can't you do anything about it?
How does anyone manage to sleep in this house at night?

Have a go, I said.
See what you can do yourself
if it troubles you that much.
Be my guest.

So he went upstairs.

He shouted at Dad,
at first quite gently, then a stentorian roar
like a bull with a china shop as big as Harrods
in its sights.
Dad didn't bat an eyelid
so Graham borrowed a megaphone,
and when that didn't work
rigged up a 500-watt Tannoy
and microphone
and told Dad what a public nuisance he was
from about a foot away.
Dad just turned over on his front.

It's worse when he lies that way,
I said when Graham came downstairs.
Here, come and have a coffee.
You learn to put up with it.
We have.

But my friend Graham's
a glutton for punishment.
He drank down his coffee, then said,
I'm going back upstairs.
I'm not being beaten by this.

So he did,
bristling with determination.

He jumped on Dad's back
and did cartwheels and press-ups,
and when that didn't work
borrowed a cricket bat and gave him
a few gentle whacks,
then brought in a gang
with their road hammer
who were working on the street outside,
and when that didn't work
took a course of karate lessons
and black-belted Dad round the bedroom.
Dad didn't bat an eyelid.
He just went on snoring.

After I'd bandaged Graham's strained arm
and given him a stiff Lucozade to recover
and generally cheered him up
Graham set back off upstairs,
bristling with even more determination.

He pulled the quilt off Dad
and tickled between his toes with the yard brush,
took out the window (it was the middle of winter),
brought in a refrigeration plant
and turned the room into an ice-box,
plugged in a dozen fan-heaters
he'd borrowed from the neighbours
for a bit of a contrast,

then when that didn't work
installed the bed in a wind-tunnel
his uncle had in his garage.
No effect on Dad.
His snores if anything grew worse.

Now look here, Graham, I said –
I was getting a bit concerned about him –
you're wasting your precious time.
You've got to accept
some people have snores louder than others.
No one snores in our house,
he said.
I don't believe in it.
I'm determined to stamp it out.

He went back upstairs
with the garden hose,
and when that didn't work
diverted the Thames through the bedroom,
and when that didn't work
borrowed a cat and dog
which chased each other all over the bed,
and a tiger from the zoo
which just snuggled down beside Dad,
and a crocodile which gave him a short back and sides.

This is getting impossible, impossible,
Graham was muttering,
I've never had to go to these extremes before –
when Mum came out of the bathroom.
She tapped Dad on the shoulder.
Hey! Stanley! she said. You're snoring again.
Dad turned over on his back.
Sorry, he mumbled. You only have to ask.

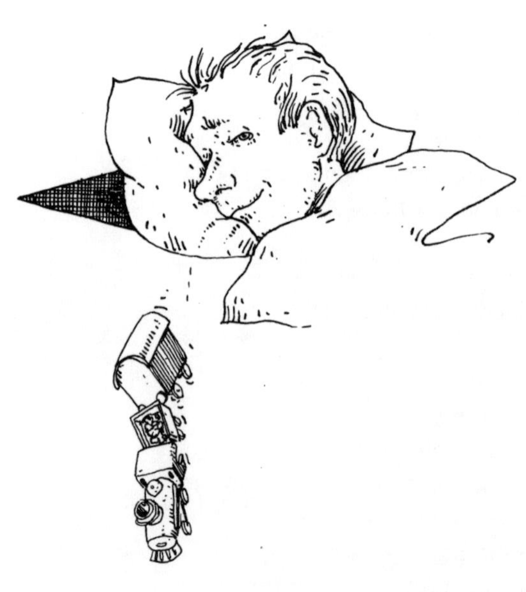

ANYBODY, NOBODY

Some children's pocket money would fill a bag or barrow.
The richest boy in the world's would fill a juggernaut.
But I just know (whatever they say) even if he is lonely,
he wouldn't want to swap places with me.

'If you don't like the hotel you know what to do!'

'Who's going to fetch that washing in from the line?'

'Someone needs to run down the chip shop.'
(Whoever saw a grown-up run to a chip shop?)

'You get it dirty so why shouldn't you – '

'You eat them so why shouldn't you – '

Won't *anyone*?
Is *nobody* going to?
I'm *who* and *someone* and *anyone* and *nobody*.

'You can have your 75p pocket money in pennies,' Dad says,
'to make it seem bigger.
Though it'll soon burn a hole in your pocket.'

'And who's going to sew it?' calls Mum.
'I was joking,' Dad shouts back. *'Nobody!'*

CORNERS OF THE NIGHT

In the box room Darren dreams of Samantha
who's invited him to the disco, not vice versa,
and he's said Yes! She'll be fetching him
on her motorbike. As luck will have it his whole class
will be passing at this very moment.

At the foot of Darren's bed the gerbil dreams
of a world in which the desert sand
isn't all sawdust and cardboard paper, and where
he does not have to sleep with a pair of socks
dangling over the mouth of his burrow.

Dad's Maserati has developed engine trouble.
Steering with his ankles he negotiates the chicane
while cleaning the carburettor with his teeth.
An oil slick sends him all ways at once
but just at the right moment the engine fires.

Mum has a lovely dream, so lovely
it makes her want to cry when she wakes for a second.
Then she realizes the alarm has not gone,
that the window is black, and with a smile
the dream enfolds her again.

Downstairs the dog dreams he's sleeping
up on Lisa's bed with her arms around him.
Lisa dreams her prize is an hour's free shopping
with ten trolleys in the toy department.
Might they change the rules – might they make it twenty?

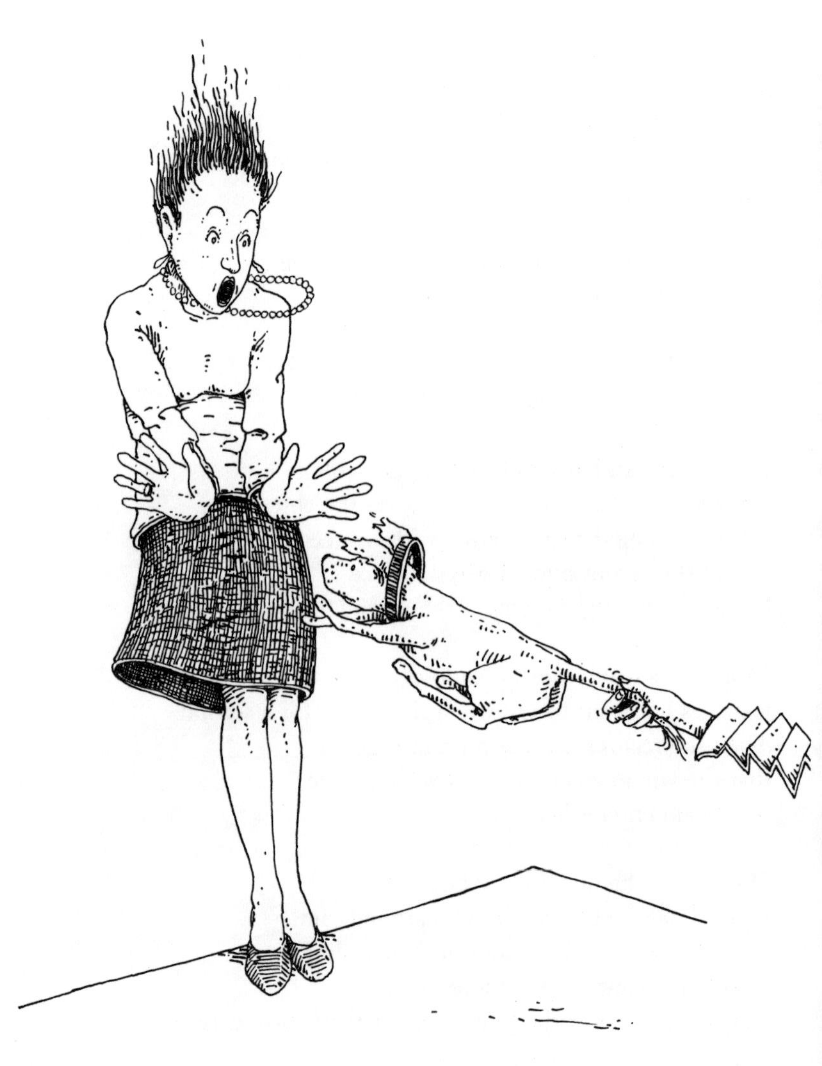

A PLAYGROUND VISITOR

The queue for the toilet starts to thin.
Suddenly everyone's chasing a dog.

How the dog loves it!
It's never had such fun in its life.
The wind streams its hair.
Its eyes bulge with excitement.
Its ears swivel like antennae.
Round and round the playground it runs,
always a tail's-length ahead of its pursuers,
slowing a paw to let them catch up
but never quite reach.
Round and round the playground,
round and round,
dizzy with excitement.

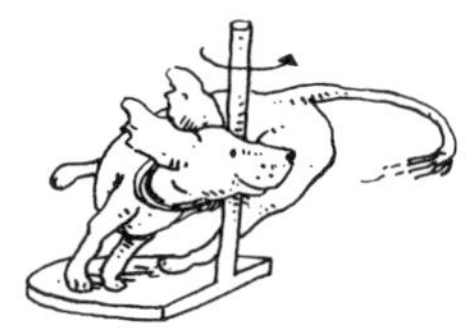

But suddenly the dog's the only one running.
It stops and wonders.
It cocks its head to one side.
Come on! Come on! it barks. *Come on!*

But now the dinner ladies are moving in,
and the teacher on duty.
They try to coax it their way.
The dog's having none of that.
It backs away, tail still wagging, barking.
It turns and begins to run at half-speed
hoping the dinner ladies will break into a canter –
tuck their skirts in and pick their knees up –
and runs, slap-bang, into a fourth-year prefect
who grabs it by the tail.

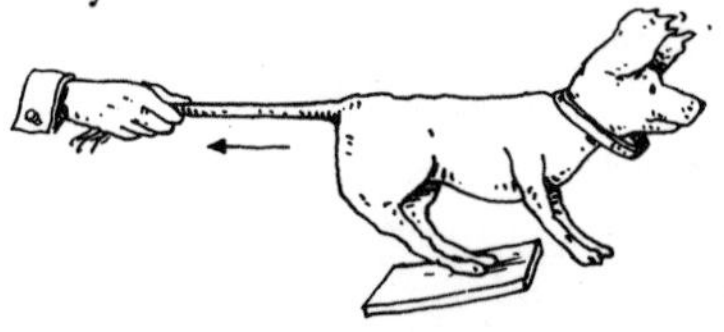

The dog yelps – and snaps.
It snaps thin air
but the prefect tumbles backwards
and cries out in fear.
Other hands try to grab the dog
but the dog swerves this way and that
through a forest of legs,
some darting towards it,
others getting away as quick as they can,
feet, legs, knees, not a forest
any longer but a vortex
of limbs and faces and voices shouting,
a mixed hue-and-cry and wail of fear.

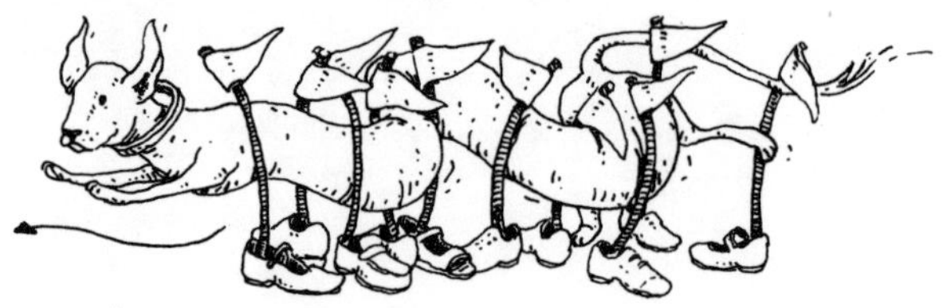

The dog cries too, whimpers,
crouches low, lips drawn back,
teeth bared in a snarl
that comes out as another whimper.
And adult hands are reaching towards it
while the dinner ladies shepherd the children –
some crying, some hysterical –
into an avenue down which
the dog is frog-marched by the collar
and expelled through the school gates
into the street.
The gate's shut
and another prefect's stationed there.

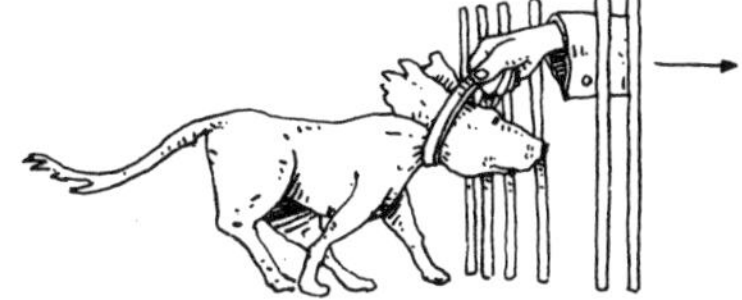

The dog shakes itself free and runs off.
That was fun, it thinks. Mostly.

Then a little voice is heard.

'That was my dog.
You were cruel to him,
all of you.'

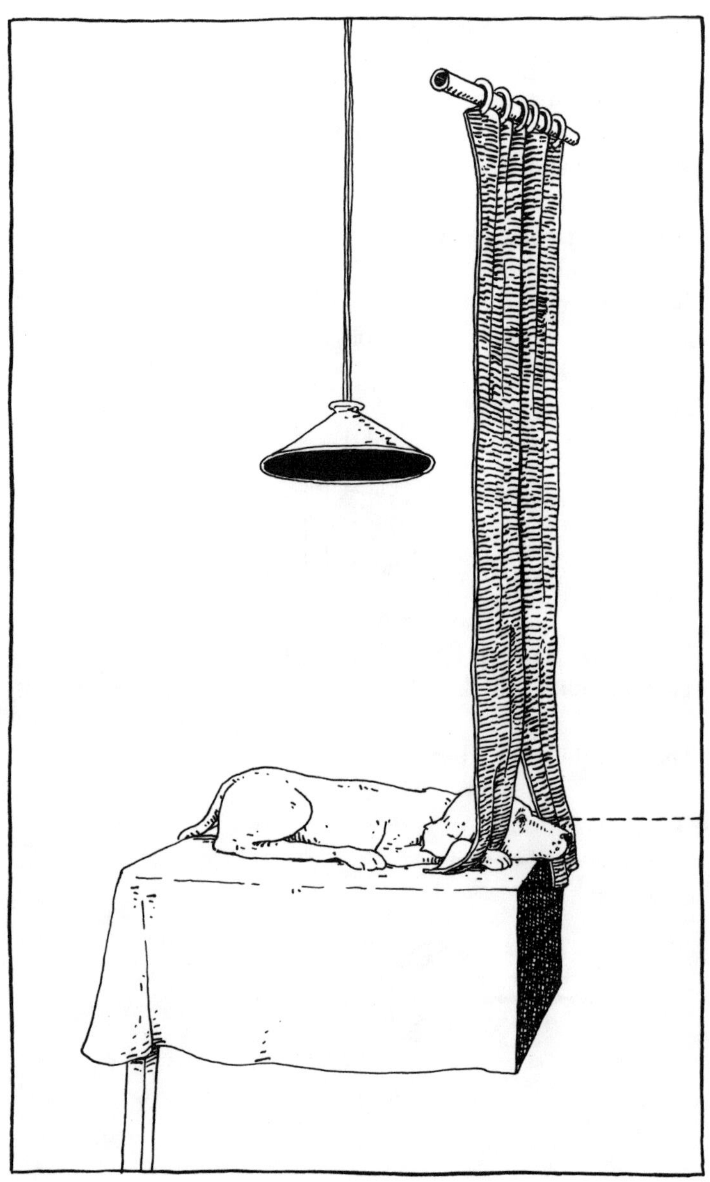

THE WORST THAT COULD HAPPEN

At lights out he howled so none of us slept.
When at last he was quiet
in the three o'clock darkness
we found him on the table
nose pressed between the curtains
eyes focused on a spot so distant
none of us could imagine it –
this unimaginable place he came from,
dumped from it on the end of the world's drive.
Stroked, he sleeps
but we are not the heroes or heroines of his dreams.

Next morning his walk became a dash for freedom.
He has not returned from it.

THE KEY CATS

My two cats Babs and Yoda follow me in
but won't follow me out.
But close a door and it's an irresistible challenge.

Anything shut away or that shuts
is a mystery,
any tin,
whatever it has in,
put an opener near it –
Purr! Stretch!
Do they purr! Do they stretch!

Babs is different –
when she curls up on my lap
all content for the moment
with the enigmas of life
she lets love lick over her.

Yoda is different –
she won't be picked up
but she strokes herself against my knee
or my hand.
All the strokes are shut in herself –
she's the one to let them out.

When I go out
they stand at the window.
You can see their thoughts in balloons.
Why aren't we out there?
What's the secret?
Where's she hidden the key?

OWL

At four in the morning, when darkness still clung to the trees and in the valley, then, as a clock shuddered, somewhere, in that dark, afar, when an icy palace seemed to break into jagged crystals, afar, in the next room, in my heart, in that dark, an owl sailed through the night. Shrieking, it rode the billows of the air, blent with the darkness of the branches, then, rising, became a stark outline against the sky. As it came nearer and nearer its cry was louder and louder. In a moment when the icy lunar glitter failed to beat, its cry passed over me, over the roof, over the dark, into nothing, leaving my mind a void, blank. Unthinking, trying to think, until five I waited. At five rain came playing on the window and concentrating on its sound I slept.

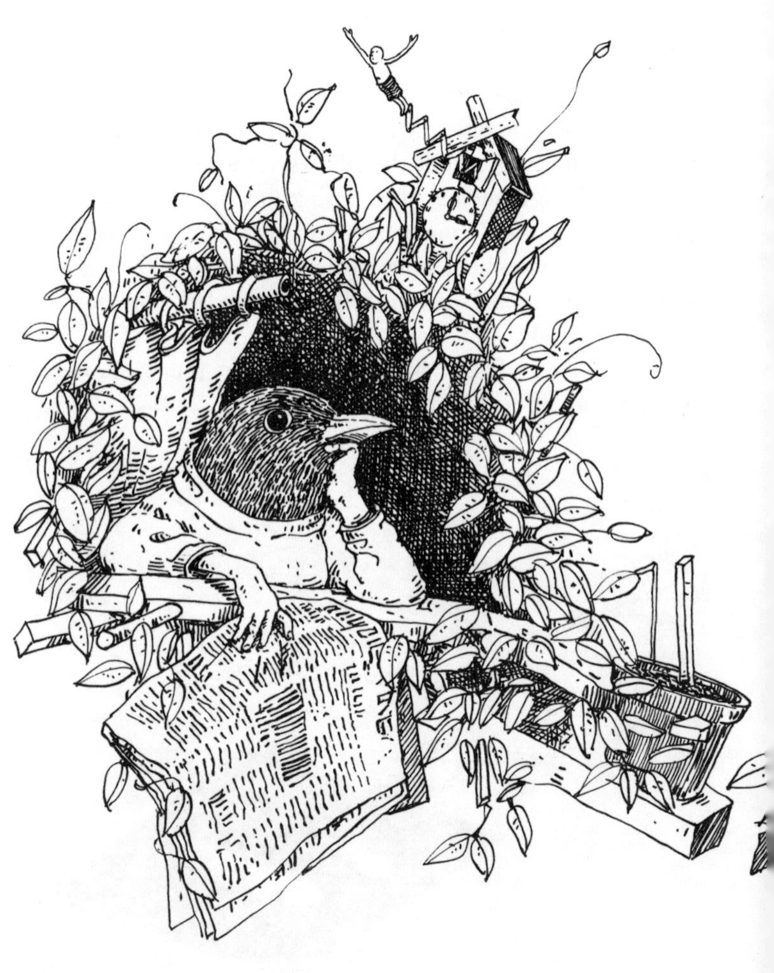

THE BLACKBIRD

From a gap in the hedge
a black hole inflated
against hail, gale, war, frost
he glares at April

Spring?
Better in the old days
Spring?
He's seen warmer Decembers
Spring?
He hawks and spits and strains his feathers

Cloud breaks
Sunshine fills the gardens

Stares stonily
Seen it all before
No fool
Don't trust it

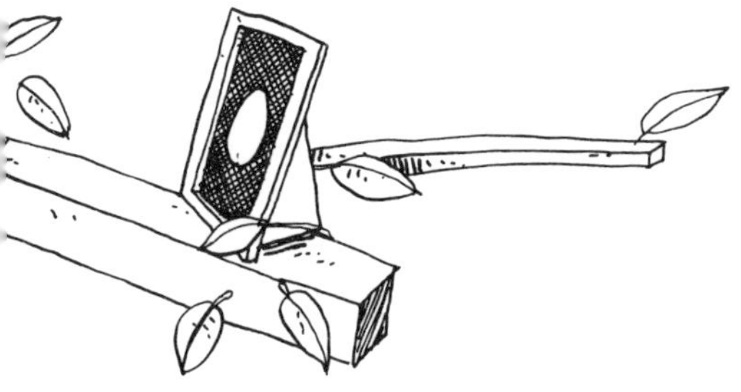

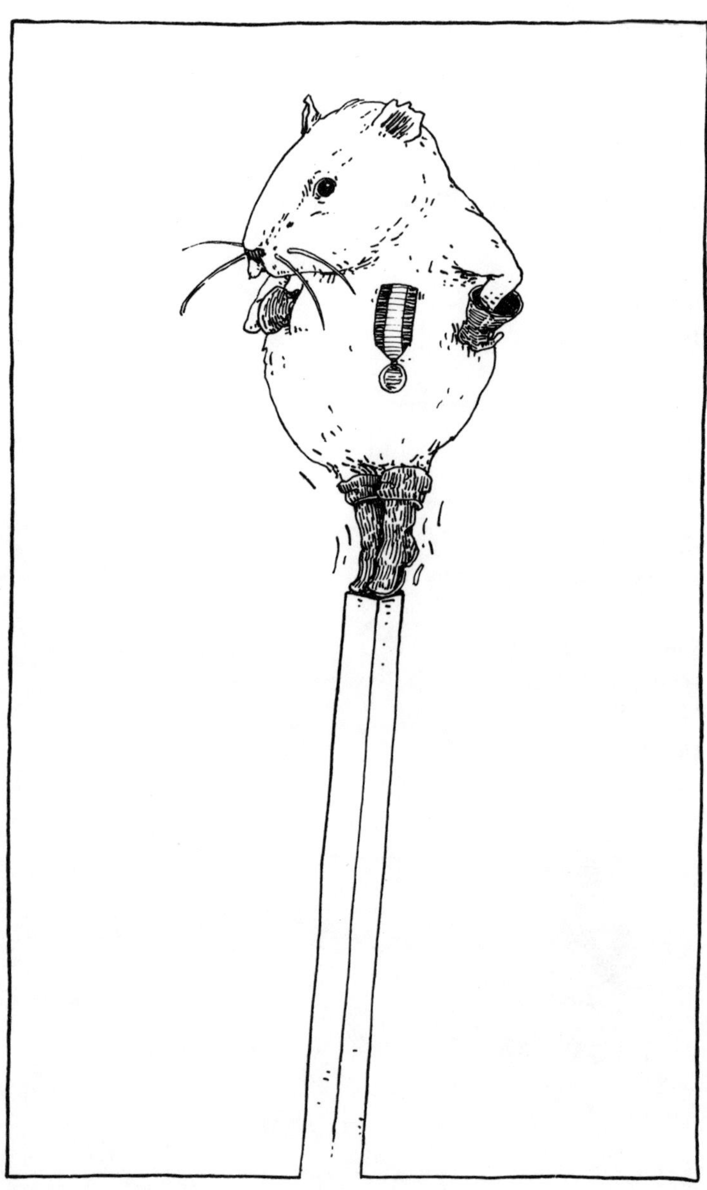

THE MEEK SHALL INHERIT

In dreams
guinea-pigs climb trees to build log cabins,
outface with their tenor the dawn chorus,
sail with Columbus to the lands of their ancestors,
lassoo in paw round up long-horned cattle,
raise hell among the pigeons.

How reassuring
to wake
with nothing to look forward to
but the long day laid out ahead
like paving-stones,
the 22p economy mix at eight,
a carrot at twelve,
hay at six,
and three times a week
the luxury of a clean cage.

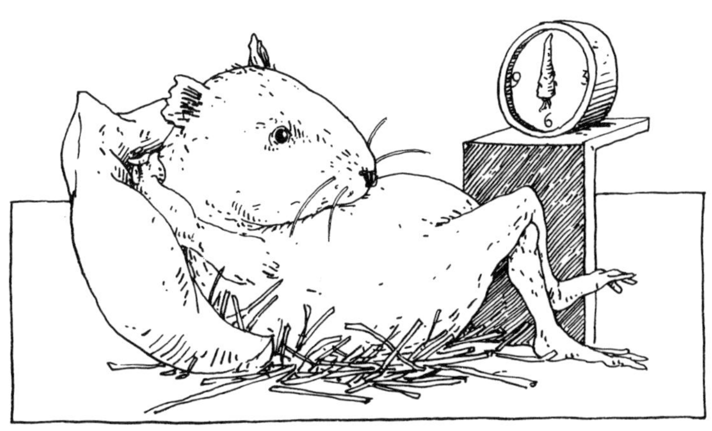

KITTEN WITH SNOW

The first flakes
come
as a surprise,
an irritation,
a ground
for protest.

Such indignity
against fur,
cold
whiteness
that clings
then dissolves
before it can be acted upon!

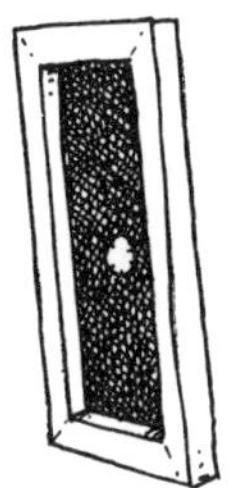

Then you get
the idea.

It is a thing
to be watched,
a wonder,
a sideshow –
though now and then
a paw
wavers
against glass,
not
quite
convinced.

THE PICNIC

A hot and dusty day.
Tommy and Alice
held hands beneath the trees.
Aunt and Uncle
and my elder cousins
laughed.
I laughed too
though the sun was hot
and the grass made me sneeze.
Just one thing spoilt my day,
a snake on the path.

In bed I could think
of nothing but snakes,
snakes in the bedclothes,
snakes on the cover,
snakes under the pillow.
And I dreamed of snakes
invading the house,
the bathroom, front room,
snakes as stair-rods,
snakes crawling from cupboards.

I woke with the light:
nothing is safe
and the house sniggers.

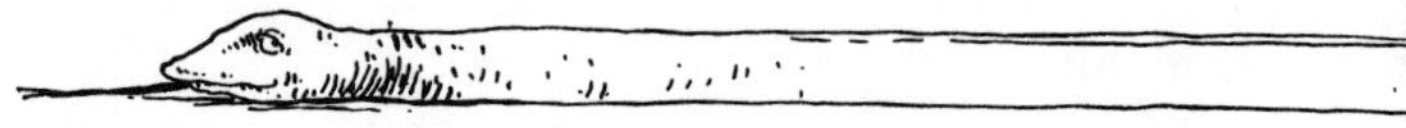

There's a gap between
the open door
and the top of the stairs
too swift for eye to see.
It's there, curled somewhere.
And the house laughs –
wide-eyed,
entranced by this thing.

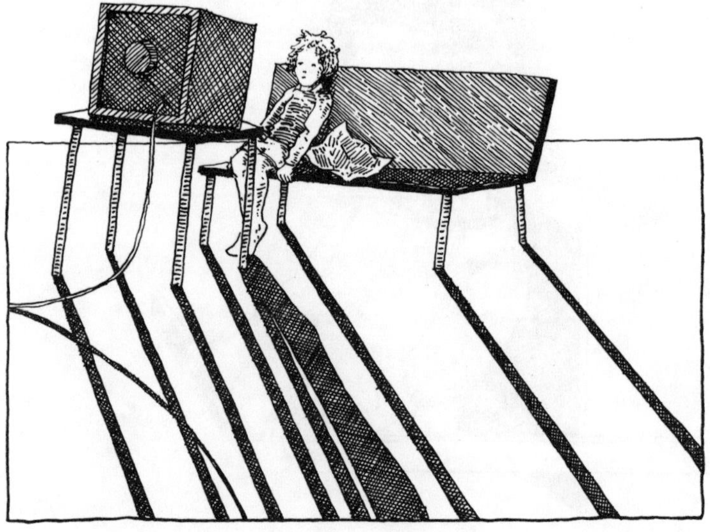

A WHISPER OF FROST

In a whisper of frost
and drift of wind,
Winter sets foot in Dagger Lane –

at about eight o'clock
of a September evening
as the sun climbs the upper windows.

In the park it scratches
the surface of the ornamental lake,
pulls a squirrel's tail,

chases a startled dog –
then leaps back north,
leaving dreams of snow

on the fingertips
of a six-month-old baby,
of the Himalayas, of icy ravines.

Suddenly the house feels
larger, more hollow.
What was that flicker on the screen?

CAT IN THE WINDOW

Cat in the window,
  what do you see?

Cloud, wind, leaves,
  a bird in a tree.

The daffodils shivering
  in the February breeze,

A puddle in the road
  beginning to freeze.

Snow on the wind,
  dusk in a cloud,

Leaves in a frenzy,
  the bird's head cowed.

Winter – though the sun shines.
  Blizzard, and the north wind's whine.

ALICE AND THE FROG

Once upon a time
a princess called Alice
dropped her golden ball
in the ornamental pond
and a nameless frog
made her make a solemn promise
before doing
his big rescue act.

At tea-time
frog hopped gamely after,
rang the bell,
jumped between the major-domo's legs,
skittered down the marble hall,
forced his way past the footmen
and croaked his challenge.

Alice's father the king
knew at once what the frog was after
(the same had happened to his elder daughter).
Despite the princess' caterwauling
he accepted the amphibian
as his future son-in-law –
Prince of *Where-Did-You-Say*?

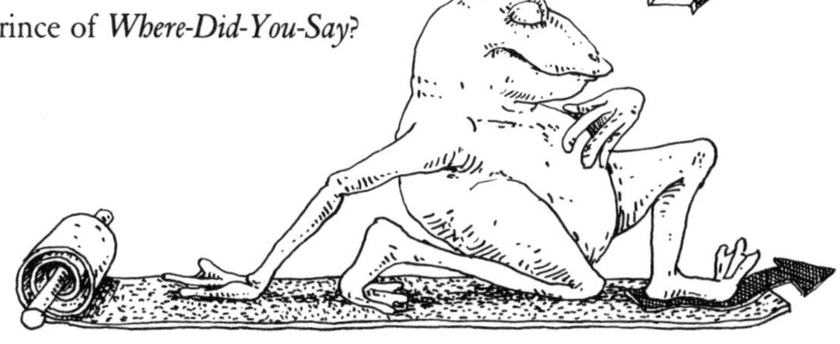

Ravenous, the frog supped keenly
and royally
on the take-away Macdonald's.
The icecream made him chilly
but the brandy went down well.
The king gazed with growing excitement at the atlas
and made him slop his pad print
on a clean sheet of headed paper.

Upstairs the frog pattered after Alice
puffed and panted into the bedroom
where the princess was taking off her make-up.
I suppose we better get this over,
she said, giving him a dry kiss,
then pushed him aside without a glance
to have a look at her bridal costume catalogue.

Downstairs Dad was packing
the royal jewels but not the debts.
You're sure Ruritania's sunny?
he said to the travel-agent
over the phone
before it was cut.
His title's good? They really have oil?
Yes, a single ticket.

Oh! and then the wedding
and the honeymoon.
Don't you wish you were here
the king's postcard says.
But Alice lies a-bed
(she nicked her finger)
the privet's growing thicker
and for the Prince
the footmen stand disconcertingly still.

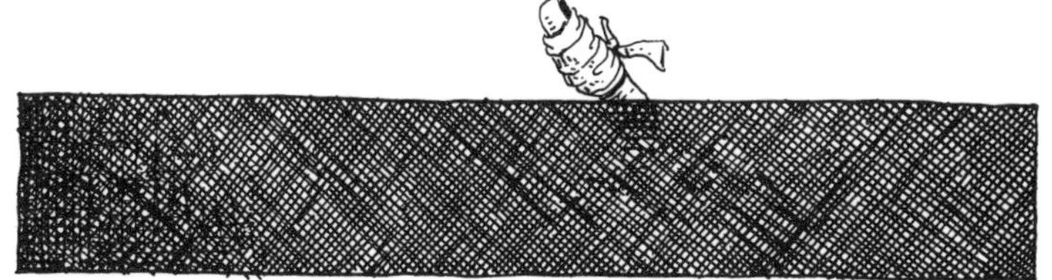

DEAR SIR

Dear Sir,
This may sound like an excuse –
for which I apologize –
but I did not realize that today's exam
was English Lit
and therefore revised my physics last night
after the late film –
though not for more than ten minutes
should you worry I wasted my time.
In any case Denise Levertov borrowed
all my English Lit books last summer
and has not yet returned them
so even if I had not been so sleepy
it would have been precious little use
and frustrating
if I had tried my best to no avail.
Last night's film was okay
and called *The Prince of Darkness*.
Even though it was in black and white
and the sound was crackly
I enjoyed it. This prince,
whose name was Hamlet, pretends
to go mad and kills his girlfriend's dad
by poking a sword through a curtain.
Sometimes I wouldn't mind getting
my girlfriend's dad behind a curtain
and sticking a sword in him
especially when he says you're both only thirteen
and a late-night as far as you're concerned
is a quarter past nine – got it, chuck?

This Prince was a really mixed-up person.
If I'd behaved like him
my mum and the headmaster
would have had me
straight down the cop-shop within five seconds
but luckily for him he lived in History,
not to mention being an aristocrat.
Funny – he talked to himself a lot,
just like the fellow in that Shakespeare
you tried to make us read last term.
Anyway, sorry again,
I see that half the class have left already.
Mr Pankhurst doesn't seem able to stop them.

Ciao, sir. Yours faithfully, Terry Atkins.

A TO Z

Rain climbs through the valley –
behind a brighter sky

Bushes thrash
aerials bend, are still
smoke hangs

Two cyclists shelter

The rain stops

How simple things are!

I imagine myself leaving
the station, walking
to your home,
a street lined with trees,
the bridge, traffic lights,
then somewhere left

Then your home

Shall I miss your number?

How simple things are!

ACROBATS

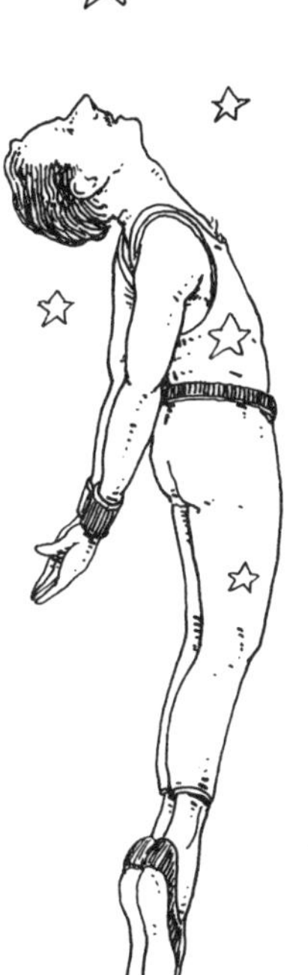

The wire takes him high
  from the sawdust
and with a pull
  he's on the platform.

The crowd look up and past
  the acrobat joining
his partner,
  steadied by her hand
on his star-dust costume,
  they see into the canvas recesses
that dwarf them
  and shock.

Now, over a gulf
  a few feet wide
and a hundred deep,
  they trick one another.
touch limbs in flight,
  landing with hands and feet
that scrabble slightly,
  bow and triumph
in this act of love.

A myth achieved, you say,
  too hard to watch?
Welcome instead, O crowd,
  the performing lions,
the bare-backed riders,
  the nonsense of the clowns!

FREE ENTERPRISE

1

Dear Draper,
Following our class's joining Pen Pal Letter Link
I have written to you
informing you that I yearn for correspondence
five times in two terms,
each time without response.
Alison Duckworth on the desk by the blackboard
has regular correspondence with Basingstoke,
Penzance, Belfast, Zimbabwe and Ohio
but out of you I haven't heard
a dicky-bird. Sonya Norton's letters
have penetrated the wastes of Western Australia
and what seemed at first a mis-match
with a princess from the Gold Coast
has led in a matter of weeks
to a class attempt to raise her dowry
of six sheep, three bullocks and a Bactrian camel
for marriage with the princess' brother –
I invite you to the bazaar
on Saturday third of May
at the Methodist Church Hall
in Wrekin Street.

Dear Draper – but what have I to show?
An address, and a name
that as time goes on
seems less and less likely.
I repeat that I am five foot four, blue-eyed,
and wear my blonde hair shoulder-length.

I enclose three photographs,
one taken in Majorca in October –
a second of the chorus line in last year's
school production of *South Pacific* –
I am near the left: you will recognize me.
The third is just a photograph,
but it was taken upon a very happy occasion.
Since my last letter I have broken off
with Peter Taylor (he was not far too old
for me as my father pontificated,
but drove too fast and was very confused
about where he was going – no pun intended).
I have had the second wisdom tooth removed –
my face was swollen for a week.
Life here remains as dry as old bones,
and I as full of nameless expectations.
Do you suffer from the same?
Write!
Love,
  Alice.

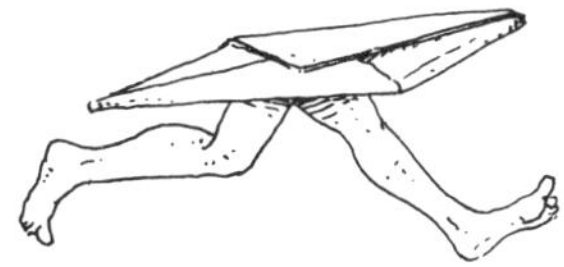

2

Dear Alice,
Some mistake must have been made –
doubtless by a computer – I can remember
the days when a computer would not have been allowed
within ten miles of a school.

I am a teacher, 38, and the coordinator
of Letter Link within this establishment.
I have not been ignoring your letters,
in fact I have been ill for nearly five months
since my wife left me
without taking the three children,
dog and mortgage – *that*
might have helped soften the blow.
Your letters intrigue, gladden and appal me.
Intrigue because what intrigues more
than the heart of a sixteen-year-old?
Gladden because after all I am more
than twice as old as you.
Appal because your candour
lays you so open.

I attended the bazaar.
You sold me three pin-cushions
and short-changed me, probably on principle.
You were more beautiful than your photographs,
but not even polite.
If I had not read your letters
I would have disliked you.
I am now severing my link with the scheme,
in fact I am severing my links with the school itself.
Love and good luck,
  Bernard.

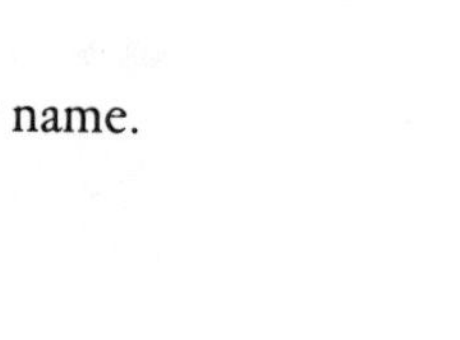

P.S.
The computer seems to have reversed my name.
My *surname* is Draper.

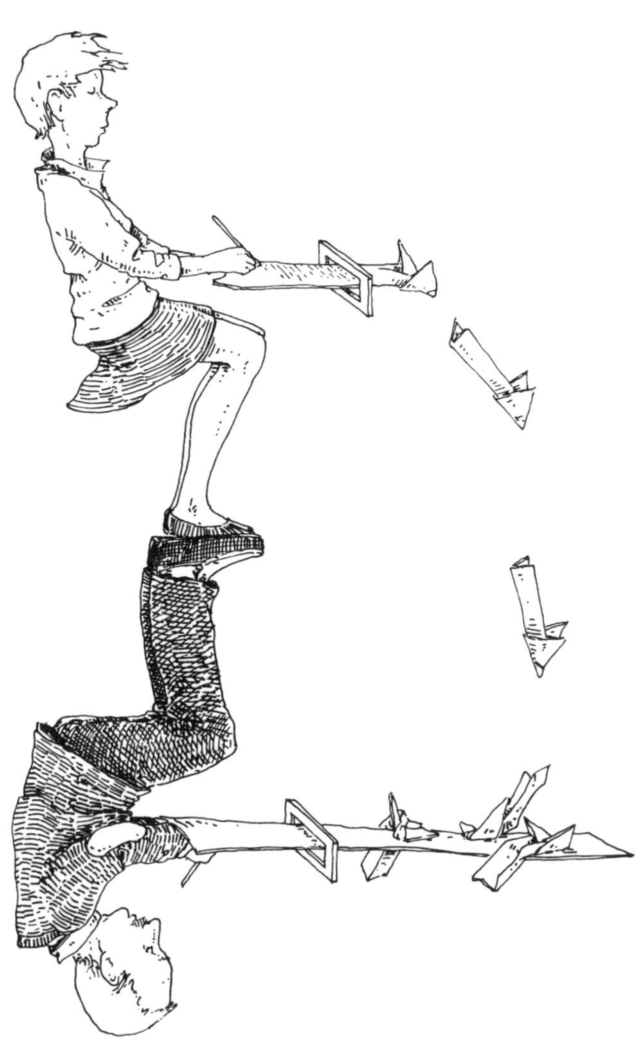

SCHOOL DAYS

'But then, as our old P.E. master, Wally,
used to say – '
Wally? Wally? Old P.E. master?
I re-found the station
and tuned it in.

'Why! I know that speaker!' I said. 'I'm sure of it.'
'Give me the *Radio Times*.
Yes, someone I went to school with,
David Hennessy. He was the year above me.
That's my old games master he's talking about!'

How it comes back! Wally!
How it comes back!
A tall hard-eyed middle-aged
whistle-swinging-on-a-cord bully
with a cropped head of hair

and a false public-school accent
underlaid with indelible cockney.
How he ruined my first and second year
Tuesdays and Thursdays!
How it comes back – the bully!

An ex-international rugby referee
even the sportsmen among us hated,
a permanent crêpe bandage on his knee-cap,
like a badge of status –
or a target.

In the second year a lad from Halesowen
deliberately head-butted the knee
during a game of pirates.
How he hopped! How he tried not to scream!
Wally never troubled him again.

'But you were eleven then, twelve,'
my wife says. 'You can't bear grudges that long.'
'Look,' I say. 'I'm sweating even now.
Feel my hands if you don't believe me.'

I thought of writing to Hennessy,
inviting him for a drink if he was ever in Birmingham.
But he'd mentioned Wally too kindly,
as if – somehow – he'd managed to get the man's measure.
No, I thought. We'd have nothing in common.
Nothing at all.

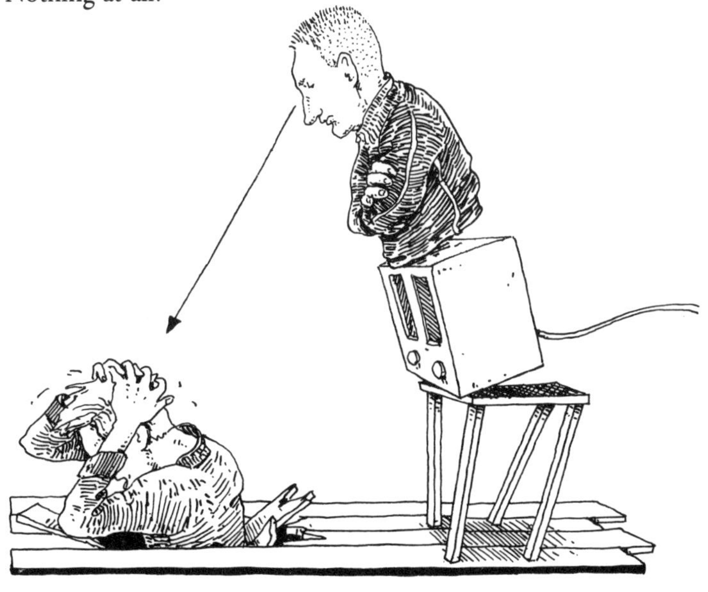

FELT TIP

The poet lies in his cot
watching the square of bright window.
'Bird!' he calls. 'Bird!' and kicks his toes.
'Listen to him!' his mother says. 'He said Mummy.'
'Daddy,' his father says. 'Definitely Daddy.'
The baby sees the wall. 'Wall!' he calls.
'Don't leave his crayons there,' his father says.
'I don't want to have to decorate again.'

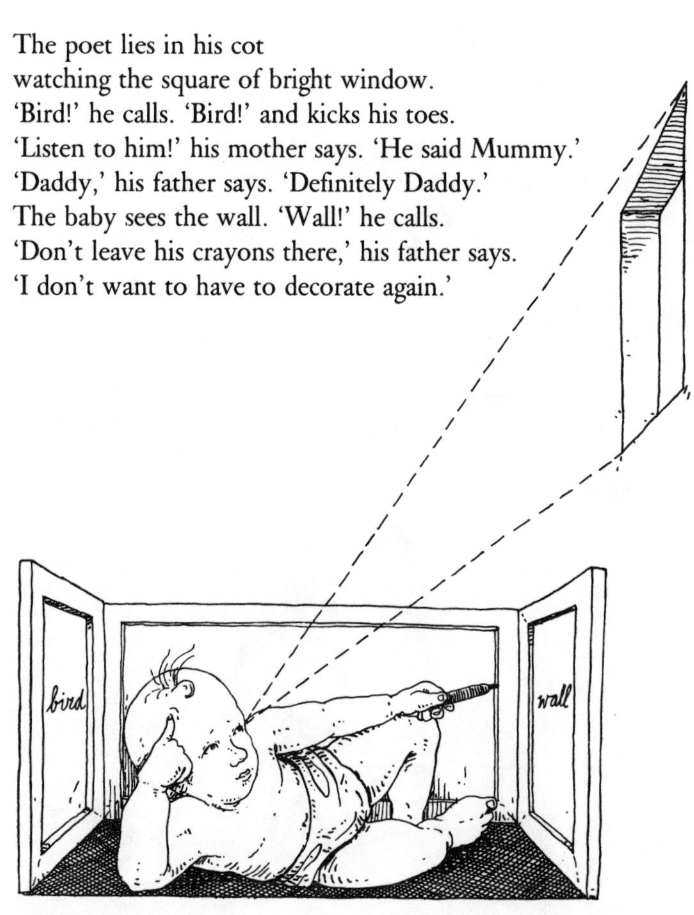

MY GRANDMOTHER POURED ME TEA

We talk about winds
because there was a high wind last night
and her memory turns that way.
It's funny to think she can remember winds
'before I was thought of'.
I ask her about Queen Victoria and she says,
'I don't go back that far, my dear.'

My grandmother
poured me tea,
one more tea
in a long line of teas.

How clearly she talks about the wind last night
and compares it with the winds of years gone by!
'And I dread the wind tonight,' she says,
disturbing me, and I ask 'Why?'
but she doesn't answer the question,
if it was a question for her.
She just blinks and goes on.

My grandmother
poured me tea,
one more tea
in a long line of teas.

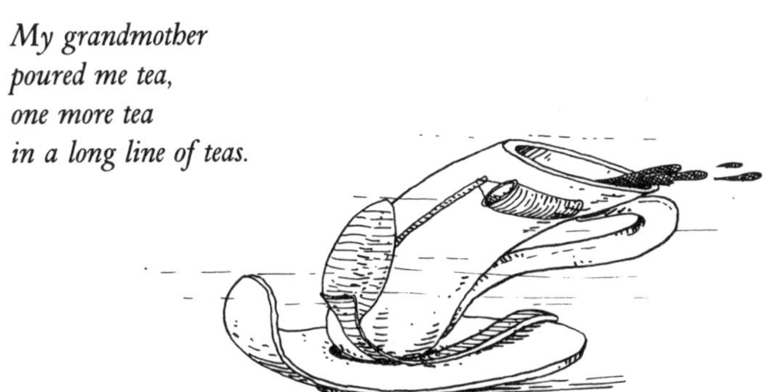

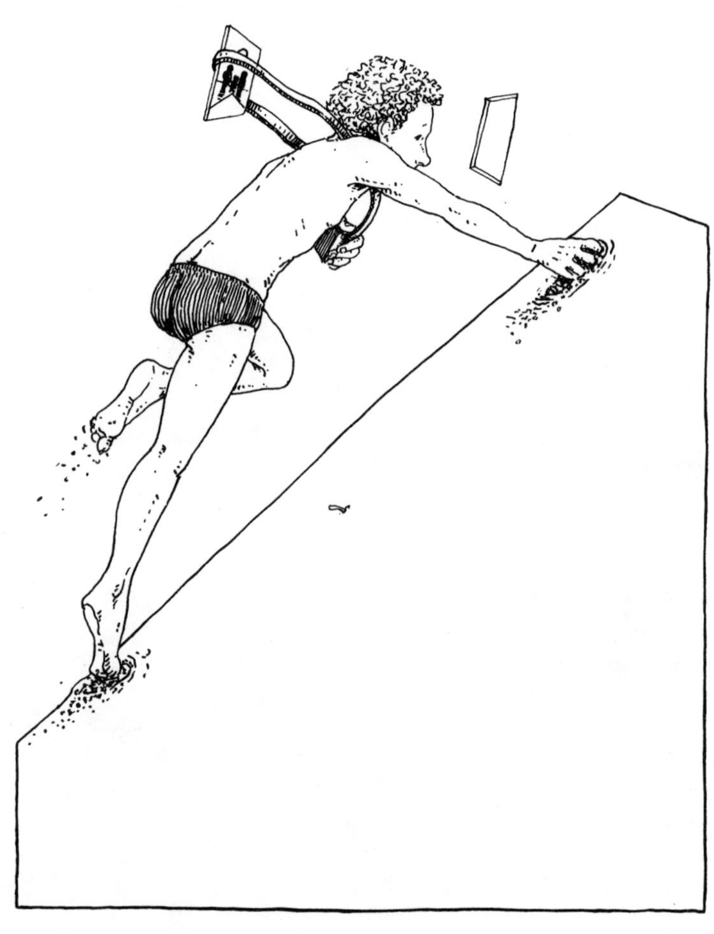

INTO THE SUN

Unconscious of my absence
they group on the sands,
gathering mats bags books,
mother father and brother,
now diminutive on the long
beach bending, always in
my sights as I climb
the dunes. Hasty I turn
beyond tall grass, gain
height, circling resee them,
drop and take them
plumb in the low sun's glare.

Still they have not seen
or lost me. I slide
bare feet burning,
white sand, pause,
circle from them (they are
admiring the sunset), reach
a gully where water still
lies, run crouching
another gully and flat
on my stomach take them,
again, unawares.

Time yet for a last look,
time to decide to forget
or remember. And how and
what to remember.

Swinging my camera
I rejoin them.

GAPPING THE GENERATIONS

'When I went to school
our desks were in rows,
and when the master came in
we stood up and said *Sir!*'
my grandfather said.

'So did we,' said my father.

'We wrote with dip-in pens
in copper-plate,
and got caned if we blotted
our copy-book,'
my grandfather said.

'More or less the same,
except we had fountains,'
said my father.

'We had respect for our elders,
none of this questioning authority,
none of this ducking responsibility.
We looked people in the eye,'
my grandfather said.

'We muttered occasionally,'
said my father.
'Otherwise ditto.'

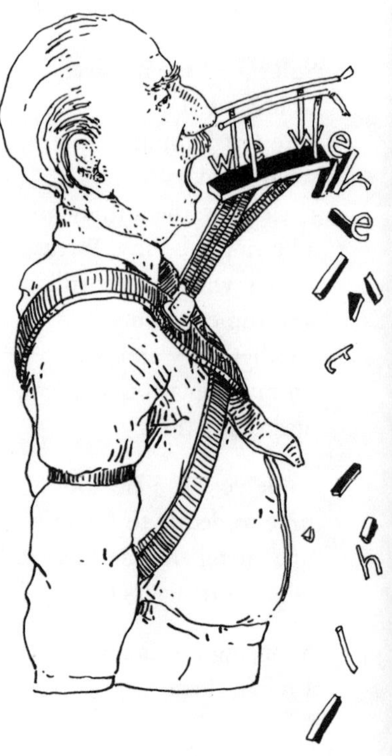

'No long-haired hippies.
No C.N.D. marches.
No rock-and-roll rubbish.
No demonstrations against apartheid.
None of this everyone equal – '

'Hey!' my father said.
'That's us you're talking about!
Not this lot!
You're twenty years out of date!
You've got the wrong generation!
Silly old goat!'

LEAVE THE STAIRS LIGHT ON

'Leave the stairs light on, please!'

I glanced up the stairs
and left it on.

Not that there could have been anything
in the bluey shadow of its straight descent –
the half-past-eight sun
four thumb-breadths above the horizon,
birds with a last threat in the garden,
cars scarcer on the road.
At least not *really* anything.

But anything? What 'anything'?

Real shadows lengthened across the garden,
took over.
Other lights switched on –

'And leave it on – remember!'

Staircases in thrillers,
dream staircases for falling,
staircases in Enid Blyton deserted houses on moor edges.

'Anything?'

Checking round the house at bed-time,
pulling curtains, switching fires,
locking, bolting – against burglars surely?
Yes – but what else? Against the door
that creaks open at one in the morning, the fumble
for the light, the scream?
What there might be under the bed?

Anything.

'Leave it on all night, please.'

EDWARDIAN NIGHTMARE

A man starts out of a forgotten nightmare – or in his dream thinks he does. Dawn, drawn curtains, mirror, wash-stand. To his right a curtained window. Light, dawn, birds singing. To his left a dark framed picture above a chest-of-drawers. An ashtray, a set of books, a sepia photograph. All normal, he thinks. All well. Time to get up. Time to go to work. The man gets out of bed. He starts for the door. But he cannot reach it. Everything seems to recede from him. Everything is out of his grasp – his dressing-gown, his slippers, the antique phone on the bedside table. Eventually he is running. The path to his door becomes a blur. When will this end? he cries. I thought this nightmare had finished.

HOMECOMING

'P' team
must have got their data
righter than they thought
for the wakening was peaceful
after the disasters of arrival at Homing.
I slid from dream
of Mary Anne and her kisses
on Labour Day last Fall
(though of course she'd be
long dead by now) to the voice
of Ship Mother saying,
'Hal, you have been asleep
for thirty years and it is time to wake.
We are approaching Earth fast.
You have tasks to perform.'
Earth on the monitor
was clouded, but on the dark side
the light of cities showed through
to welcome us.
I could already
smell the morning mist
on the slopes of Mount Kirk
(Planet Homing had been flat
beyond monotony). Sleepy-eyed
we greeted each other
in the captain's cockpit
briefly, a hand-shake, a kiss
on the cheek for the ladies, and
spread out through the vessel to our posts.
It was Trypanis first voiced it,

puzzled on the intercom, 'An anomaly,
something's not quite right here.
I can't quite put my finger on it.'
'Will it kill us?' – that was Kieran,
urgent, a little too fast on the ball –
'or cripple the ship? No?
In that case we're too far committed
to abort. It's now or never.
Landing in three Earth minutes.
End of a long journey, folks.
Goodbye and hello.
Hope they're still friendly.'
Earth came up to greet us.

The citation of the President
speaks of bravery, endurance, excellence,
history, future, family, public,
but it's Trypanis's words haunt.
This is Earth?
Our Earth? Was the Ship Mother
cleverer or dumber than we suspected?

A DAY ON THE PLANET
or Invasion Thwarted
The School Trip that went Right

For Alan Tucker

To The Supreme Commander, Sirian Forces,
Solar System

Hail!
Greetings!

We landed, ten and a half hours local time,
at the large habitation, Weston Manor, our spy-ship
reconnoitred in the middle of last Terran winter.
However conditions had changed and
instead of being deserted the grounds were occupied
by a large number of Young Earthlings
being moved about in classes or 'showers'
as they are referred to by the smaller number
of Adult Earthlings who were leading them.

At first it was thought to have become
a correction centre with the young creatures
('school children' as they are called)
being exercised or punished in this random fashion
but we later realized that, on the contrary,
it was the Older Earthlings
(or 'school teachers' as they are called)
being tested or examined.
These school teachers seemed inoffensive
but were armed with weapons such as
'detentions' and 'lines' and 'tell your parents'
which, however, were concealed about their persons.

Taking upon ourselves our disguises
we infiltrated the house
which we found was also occupied by the school children.
They were everywhere and being shouted at
by a different species of school teacher called 'guides',
mainly ill-tempered older women in tweed skirts
with immaculately groomed grey hair,
who expostulated nauseatingly upon
the supposed glories of the Manor,
its pictures, carpets and furniture,
at the same time issuing constant commands
'Not To Touch!'.

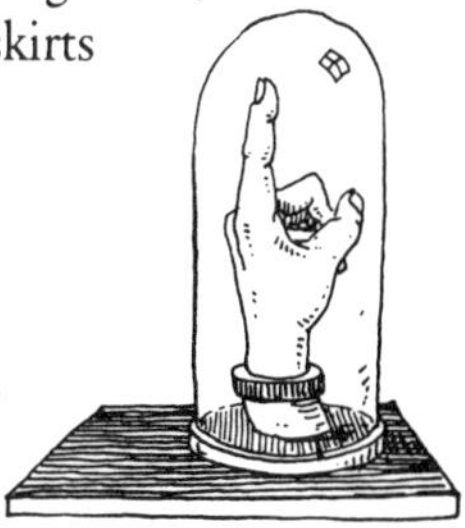

This made us realize there was danger in these objects
so we abandoned our intention of placing the M.U.S.P.MO.
(Mark IV Ultra Sonic Population Subjugation Module)
on the chair in the dining room
(this Chippendale must be a powerful magician
to command such respect –
if nothing else is learnt from Earth I humbly suggest
we at least investigate the source of his power).
We left it instead on the floor in the entrance hall,
a mistake for it was immediately spotted by an 'idiot'
(singular of 'school children')
who pocketed it.
The idiot no sooner had it in his possession
than he was grabbed by an inside teacher
who told him in a loud whisper
'if there was any more malarkey'
he would be 'out on his neck'
(another terrible Earth punishment).
(On our preliminary visit we, of course,

had no direct contact with the dominant species
especially this aggressive sub-group.)
We assumed appropriate disguises and followed,
though our next glimpse of the M.U.S.P.MO.
came only when the idiot engaged in
bartering it for a bag of something that appeared edible.

There followed a bewildering series of exchanges
in which the Subjugation Module changed pockets
at least ten times, finishing by being exchanged
for a small round coloured glass object,
the purpose of which was not ascertained.
Not only, however, did it pass from one idiot
to another but also from shower to shower.
Twice it was taken back into the house
(the inside teachers were by now even more aggressive –
on a scale from 1 to 7 they were 6.3 and rising).
Finally one of the school teachers (or 'berks')
spotted it being thrown from idiot to idiot
and 'confiscated' it.

Fearing the worst of this 'confiscated' we assumed
even more appropriate disguises.
The school teacher examined, then attempted to open it
with a screwdriver – happily it resisted
all his frenzied assaults,
but remained in his pocket
as he marched his shower here and there
from what he called one 'attraction' to another
until tiring of this game, or perhaps having passed –
or failed – his test (it was difficult to decide which)
he led the school children
to a large multi-windowed motor vehicle
in which another shower was already seated.
We made a last attempt at retrieval.

I ordered storm-trooper Markee
to assume an appropriate disguise
and follow the M.U.S.P.MO. onto the 'coach'
(name of the vehicle).
Unfortunately this began to move off
almost immediately.
The last we saw of Markee
(his emergency beacon continued to broadcast distress calls
for a quarter of an Earth hour)
he was being passed from idiot to idiot
in the backseat of the coach
while being waved with considerable loss of dignity
to the accompaniment of raucous cheers
at the occupants of other coaches.
Random aggression readings on the charge-persons
of these coaches deterred any attempts at following –
any attempt to recover the M.U.S.P.MO. or Markee
would have led to considerable loss of life.
We therefore left Earth
and forward this preliminary report
as we return with all haste to the Mother Vehicle.

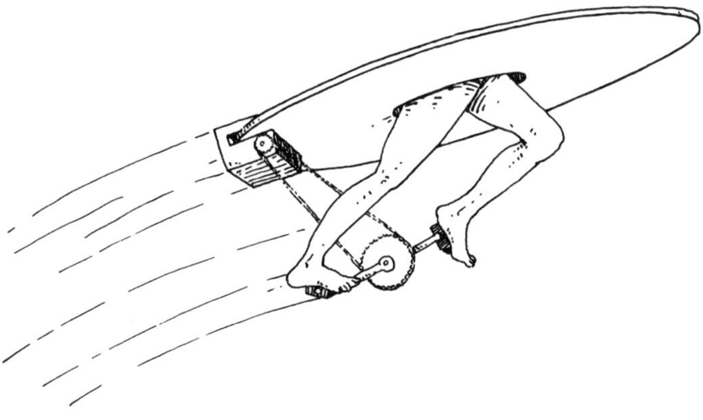

A MARTIAN VISITOR

Dawn! So this is dawn!
How beautiful, the Martian visitor said
adjusting his antennae.
No.
Merely breakfast and bathroom lights
and traffic scurrying towards the city.
For dawn,
cast your eyes up
and towards the horizon.
Ah, where I come from,
he said.

And those are flowers, and fields, and woods?
Your landscape is famous Solar System wide.
No.
You have mistaken
the advertising billboards
and the municipal park.
Those trees are streetlights.
Those trees are trees.
The flowers are lower down.
Ah yes I understand.
My guide-book is evidently out of date,
he said.
I must rewrite it.

I have been studying your advertisements,
he said later that day
with some excitement,
and I have discovered
something my guide-book did not well explain.

Love. I have discovered Love.
It is a machine that spins white clothes,
a brown liquid in a brimming jar,
a short stick between pursed lips.
I will write an article
extolling its virtues
when I return to Mars.
How romantic Earth is!
He took his notebook out.
Will you marry me? Ah – I thought not.
Could I have your reasons?

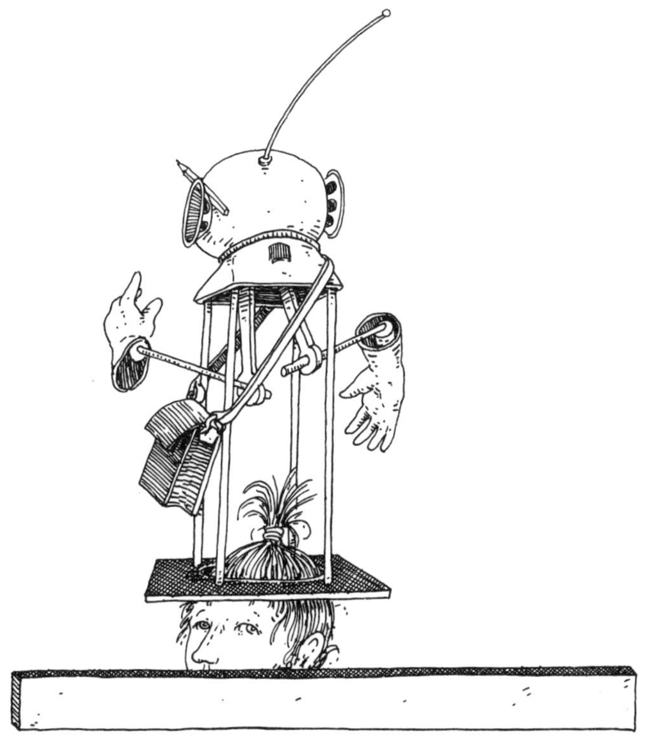

PICNIC ON THE MOON

A picnic on the moon
  is a silent affair
    as absence of air
      is unconducive
        to serious conversation.

Sandwiches on the moon
  drift out of reach,
    hilarious the first time,
      funny the second.
        The pollution robot has been programmed
          to retrieve them.

Football on the moon
  is impossible.
    All ball-games are equally impossible,
      baseball, cricket, snooker.
        The okey-cokey is banned.

And when the party's over,
  then it's time to face
    the blue-and-green orb
      floating in the ethereal blackness,
        tug of Earth Mother
          lost for ever.

'Gather possessions.
It is time to depart,'
intones the robot-guide
over the intercom.
'The solar winds are turning.
Gather possessions.'

After each departure
the moon-mice come out to play
'Our grandparents saw the explosions,' they twitter.
'They saw the explosions.
What did they mean? What did they mean?'

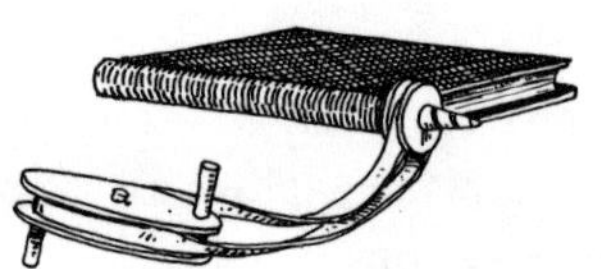